JOURNEY

Anger Management with Spiritual Principles

Marvin Price Jr.

Table of Contents

Unless otherwise indicated, all Scripture quotations are taken from the *King James Version* of the Bible.

Direct quotations from the Bible appear in quotation marks.

Journey - Anger Management with Spiritual Principles
ISBN – 13: 978-0692 440865
Copyright ©2010 by Marvin Price Jr.

Emotional Trials

Step 1. Cycle of Indecision

Step 2. Choice

Step 3. Rationalization

Step 4. Love

Step 5. Control

Step 6. Truth

Step 7. Self-Created

Step 8. Pride

Step 9. Fear

Step 10. Loneliness

Step 11. Inferiority

Step 12. Applying new insights

Introduction

Welcome and thank you for taking the opportunity to gain a new spiritual perspective towards anger and the emotions associated with it. I was inspired to bring to light the dangers of living with unresolved anger both from my personal life experiences as well as the experience gained from helping others in crisis during my professional career as a family counselor. More importantly, gaining an understanding of how to apply biblical principles not only greatly benefited my quality of life, but also those whom have shared their testimonies after completing this twelve-step program.

Journey's Objective

Journey's objective is to empower and encourage the reader to take an insightful look at the destructive impact that unresolved anger has had within their life. Accept responsibility for their role in allowing the anger to control their behavior, and apply new spiritual insight towards improved coping, socialization, emotional expression and quality of living.

It's the authors' desire that the reader will be able to identify learned patterns of thinking related to their anger emotion and the adverse behavioral effects and to become able to demonstrate improved decision making through applying the biblical principles to enhance their quality of living.

Self-Awareness

FYI: Truth plays a major role in the recovery process and will help you to accomplish our objective to appropriately manage our anger.

Check the statements that apply to you.

__ I often start something but never finish.

__ I get quiet when I'm upset.

__ When disappointed, I isolate myself from others.

__ I enjoy being miss understood.

__ If someone is having more success than me, I become envious.

__ I avoid people I don't like.

__ I never apologize.

__ I don't accept others opinions well.

__ I can forgive, but never forget.

__ I find myself interrupting others during conversation, not letting them complete their thoughts.

__ I sometimes blame others for my problems.

__ People often refer to me as being sarcastic towards others.

__ Quitting, runs in my family.

__I struggle with people that I feel have control of my life.

__I smile on the outside, while feeling worried on the inside.

__At times I struggle with moods of depression or discouragement.

__ It's easy for me to get into arguments, even when I try to avoid them.

__ I tend to treat people indifferently if I think that they have less than me.

__I have been known to take an "I-don't care" attitude toward the needs of others.

__ I don't like abiding by authority.

If you checked ten items, anger may be more constant in our life than you might like. If you checked fifteen or more, this may indicate that you are vulnerable to extreme ill effects of anger, rage, guilt, bitterness, un-forgiveness and resentment.

Date Completed:

_____

Return to this assessment after completing the text, to reflect on our personal growth and development as it relates to applying newly learned skills and principles towards managing our anger emotions.

Part One:
Identifying Our Anger

Identifying with Anger

Before you can begin the process of identifying with our type of anger, you must understand its meaning:

Anger is a normal emotion with a wide range of intensity, from mild irritation and frustration to rage. It is a reaction to a perceived threat to ourselves, our loved ones, our property, our self-image, or some part of our identity. Anger is a warning bell that tells us that something is wrong. You will learn that anger can actually be helpful in self-defense and in standing against unrighteousness, and can be safely expressed to the person you're angry towards.

Everyone experiences anger, and it can be healthy. It can motivate us to stand up for ourselves and correct injustices. When we manage anger well, it prompts us to make positive changes in our lives and situations.

Mismanaged anger, on the other hand, is counterproductive and can be unhealthy. When anger is too intense, out of control, misdirected, and overly aggressive, it can lead to poor decision making and problem solving, create problems with relationships and at work, and can even affect our health.

Often, the unhealthy anger emotion can enter a person's life in some of the most unthought-of ways and one of them is **indecision.** The inability to make a decision or wavering between two or more possible courses of action.

(Figure 1.1) **Cycle of Indecision** demonstrates stages that a person is most likely to go through that could potentially cause, what you'll discover in Step 7, Self-Created anger.

Cycle of Indecision

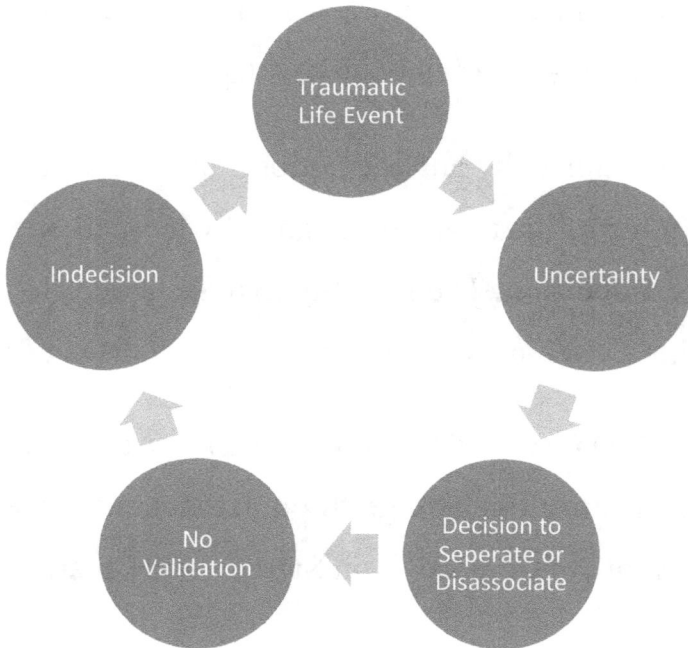

Figure 1.1

(1st) A **Traumatic Life Event** takes place in the person's life and the well-being is at stake. **(2nd)** Personal decisions become necessary to achieve well-being and **Uncertainty** associated with the need for change surface. **(3rd)** The **decision to separate and the action of separating** begins. The person takes action and begins the process of committing to the decision to separate. **(4th)**

Attempts to convince others that the need for change is met with **invalidation and opposition.** (5th) The person, influenced by not being validated or supported about their decision, then **begins to waiver about their decision** to remove themselves from the cause of their trauma. Potentially, **returning back to the conditions that created the initial trauma** that triggered their Life Changing Event.

Step 1. Is Anger a Sin?

God instructs you, in the following principle, to find a balance within our anger emotion when the emotion is connected to an issue that requires choosing a proper response (Ephesians 4:26*) "Be ye angry, and sin not: let not the sun go down upon our wrath: Neither give place to the devil. "* With this being said, the question: <u>Is anger a sin</u>? Can then be answered with the following response: Anger is not sinful, but the choices after becoming angry can lead to a sinful choice. (James 4:17) reinforces that it is the action of the person that places them in danger of committing sin, *"Therefore to him that knoweth to do good, and doeth it not, to him it is sin."*

To begin to create this balance, you must be able to identify three primary areas that affect our quality of life: (1) preservation of our personal worth, (2) essential needs, and (3) personal morals.

1. **Preserving Personal Worth:**

Anger is ignited when the person perceives or feels rejection or invalidation. Whether or not that is the message intended the person feels that their dignity has been demeaned.

So often the focus is on the message of invalidation and the person that's angered forgets about their God given worth or value. Spiritual connectedness offers great hope to those whose worth is not acknowledged by other people. It's taught that God places high value on each person who calls on Him. Even when that person fails to live perfectly, that worth is not erased.

Psalm 139:14 states: *"I will praise thee; for I am fearfully and wonderfully made: marvelous are thy works; and that my soul knoweth right well."*

Accepting our worth is a choice, even when another person chooses not to. This choice has a great effect on the intensity of the person's angry emotions. By choosing to accept our God given worth, anger will be less affective in our life.

2. Preserving Essential Needs:

People have basic survival needs; example, you are told to (Gal. 5:4) love thy neighbor as thyself, (Gal. 6:2) *"bear one another's burdens, and so fulfill the law of Christ"*. These principles recognize our complicated system of needs that must be satisfied if you're to have emotional well-being. Often, a person that struggles with anger becomes tired of having to live without their basic needs being recognized by others and begin to accuse others of no understanding who they are.

When our essential needs are not appropriately addressed or you feel invalidated, the result can lead to emotional unrest.

3. Preserving Basic Morals

A fine line exists between knowing when to stand firm for our morals and when to embrace the imperfections you see in others. There will be times in our life when it will be necessary for you to take a firm stance for our morals. Matt 21:12-13 and Mark 11:15-19, both describes

Jesus reaction to people disrespecting the purpose of God's temple. The principle here is that asserting yourself in a manner that will get the attention of others to make the point that you will not compromise when it comes to preserving our morals.

Step 2. Choices When Angered

Once you have learned to identify anger and understand its meaning, you can learn to distinguish right and wrong ways of managing it. Although you may not always like the truth about our anger, <u>you can make choices</u> about how you handle it. (Deut 31:19) *"I call heaven and earth to record this day against you, that I have set before you life and death, blessings and cursing: therefore <u>choose</u> life, that both thou and thy seed may live:"* This passage is encouraging the reader to make a decision that's going to best enhance or improve their quality of life.

There are several general choices made to manage anger when it occurs. We chose to: (1) suppress, (2) become combative, (3) passively, (4) positively, or (5) letting the anger go.

1. Silent Anger:

Many people hesitate to admit their own anger never wanting to appear worried or upset, so they maintain an image of never having problems associated with anger. This type of person usually put on a good front and pretends to feel no tension at all. They say things like; "I never get mad", "nothing upsets me," and "everything is just fine," or "I've never had a problem with anger."

2. Combative Anger:

This type of anger emotion involves preserving personal worth, needs and morals (morals) but includes intimidation, blame, bickering, and criticism, and in extreme cases physical outburst. This type of person is ready or inclined to fight. Often associated with this type of anger emotion the individual is too focused on personal imperfections of others coupled with masking their own deep personal insecurities.

3. Passive Anger:

Like open aggression, this type of anger does involve preserving personal worth, needs and morals (morals) at someone else's expense. However, it's expressed oppositely, the person refuses to fly off the handle or become verbally or physically abusive.

Passive aggression is caused by a need to have control with the least amount of directness. This type of person would typically sabotage the person that they are angry with in an effort to avoid having to confront them face to face.

4. Positive Anger:

If anger is defined as preserving personal worth, needs, and morals, then positive anger means this type of person is confident in opinion or assertion; fully assured: and considers the needs and feelings of others. This means there can be times when it's healthy to address concerns about personal worth, needs and morals, but it should be done in a manner that keeps the door open for ongoing love. (Prov. 27:5) *"Open rebuke is better than secret love."*

5. Letting the Anger Go:

Letting go is the most difficult choice to make. There are times when applying assertive anger doesn't work and one of our options is to choose to drop our anger, or let it go.

Warning: (Matt 5:22*)* stresses the importance for dropping anger; *"But I say to you, whosoever is angry with his brother without cause shall be in danger of judgment:"*

Part Two:

Anger Thrives on Unmet Needs

Step 3. Choosing to Stay Angry

When you create reasons to hold on to anger, in spite of all of the advice that you've received from others, you chose to disregard personal responsibility and hide behind self-created excuses. (Proverbs 21:2) *"Every way of a man is right in his own eyes: But the Lord pondereth the hearts."*

Here are a few rationalizations or reasons that are most common for choosing to hold on to anger:

Having a Past:

The environment that you were either born into or have chosen to be a part of can have an influence in our emotional well-being. Some people can link most of their emotional pain and unhealthy decisions to experiences of their past. Most commonly, they can recall having to endure dealing with their parent's unpleasant anger, and eventually growing up having similar experiences in their lives with spouses, relatives, children and friends.

While its necessary to "work through" past pain however, many people allow themselves to become so obsessed with the past that it becomes almost impossible for them to move forward in their life.

To get beyond a painful past you experience you must accept and acknowledge our inability to "control others" (see page 27), particularly when the experiences are permanent. You can move forward! It's more helpful for you to accept that you can't control the past, but you can choose a new direction for yourself.

Forgiveness Is Too Good:

Often, choosing to forgive seems as if you're conceding to defeat, so you hold on to the anger because forgiveness seems to let the person off the hook too easily. Let's look at some of the benefits of choosing to forgive:

- You accomplish a sense of relief and peace
- Restored relationships
- Spiritual growth and accomplishment

It is important to remember that God never ask you to do something harmful to yourself when he instructs you to forgive because He loves you enough to guide you in the way of holiness. A clean slate with God can become our motive for forgiveness. (Matt 6:14-15) *"For if you forgive men their trespasses, our heavenly Father will also forgive you: But if forgive not men their trespasses, neither will our Father forgive our trespasses".*

Why should you try when no one else is?

Have you ever been willing to apologize, or make apologies only to be rejected?

Normally, when you expect "fairness" as a requirement to help you manage anger, you're asking for trouble. You want to resolve the problem; however, in light of the other person's stubbornness you remain stuck in our anger, waiting for that person to sincerely accept our apology. This could be a problem of unhealthy dependency allowing our emotions to be too closely connected to the other person's response, causing you to lose our initial motivation to genuinely forgive the individual. At this point, you may need to ask yourself, "Am I genuinely ready to forgive?"

Holding Anger is Easier than letting go:

Just as you can get hooked on alcohol or drugs you can become hooked on anger. Going back to it again and again simply because it's a familiar part of our routine and you have found success in getting our needs met, although temporarily.

Holding on to anger can be characterized by (1) open aggression or (2) passive aggression techniques, or (3) "Bullying" to gain or maintain control over others that you perceive to be weaker than yourself. If you were able to identify with the previous mentioned characteristics you may be caught in this pattern of behavior.

Throughout the remainder of this process of exploring anger emotions: No matter what our background or circumstance, you will learn that you have a choice in the direction of our emotions. And while our emotions can be influenced by our background, you still have a responsibility before God to decide if you will let Him guide our emotions.

Step 4. The Wrong Kind of Love?

Of all of the common human needs, the most obvious and important is the need for love. However, when you lack love, you respond to our feelings of rejection with some form anger. In many cases insufficient love creates emotional instability, causing you to feel left out or un-affirmed and rejected (1 John 4:8) *"He that loves not knows not God; for God is Love."* This principle reflects the expectations that God has placed upon everyone and the benevolence that should be expressed towards others.

Being hugged and told, "I love you" is enough to satisfy our need to some degree. But that's just part of it. The following are some examples of appropriate expressions of love:

- Discipline is administered with fairness without anger. (Hebrews 6:6) *"For whom the Lord loves*

He Chastens, and scourges every son whom He receives."

- Time is spent together in reading, singing, talking, sharing thoughts & ideas. (Deut 6:7*) "And you shall teach them diligently to our children, and shall talk of them when you sit in our house, and when you walk by the way, and when you lie down, and when you rise up."*

- Taking a child's point of view into account, when big decisions within the family are being considered. (Mark 10:14-15) *"Allow the little children to come to Me, and forbid them not: for of such is the kingdom of God. Verily I say to you, whosoever shall not receive the kingdom of God as a little child, he shall not enter therein."*

(Questionnaire):

Think about our childhood as you respond to the following statements.

- Our family conversations (for instance, are open and friendly; didn't take place and or stressful)

  _____

  _____

- When I was disciplined in my home I felt (for instance, sad but still loved; or afraid and humiliated)

  _____

  _____

- I used to wish my parents would take more interest in (for instance, my education; recreational activities; spending more time together)

  _____

  _____

- Touch in my family was (for instance, all the time and odd; rare and uncomfortable)

  _____

  _____

- In major family decisions my opinions mattered or didn't matter that much. (for instance, non-existent; valued)

_____

_____

Within some families, the verbal expression of the word love never existed because some parents believed that love was implied because you were provided with food, adequate shelter and clothing. While in other families, love was expressed constantly not only verbally but also through healthy touch/hugs, and activities that included all of the family members.

Each person within the family has or developed various ways to express love. Although, the affirmation of being loved by siblings, friends and family members is considered an essential need, it's not always going to be expressed in the fashion that you desire leading to the feeling of being rejected.

Imbalanced Love Dependency

Dependency of love can allow inner thoughts and emotions to be dictated by external circumstances making you more vulnerable to an anger emotion. Healthy dependency of love is the glue that holds relationships together and strongly influences personalities. The principle within (1 John 3:23) suggest that a healthy love dependency is a commandment of God; *"And this is His commandment, That we should believe on the name of His Son Jesus Christ, and love one another, as He gave us commandment."*

Imbalanced love dependency as described in the principle of (1 John 2:15-17) warns against unhealthy attachments to material things and against strong desires towards people; *"Love not the world, neither things that are in the world. If any man loves the world, the love of God the Father is not in him. For all that is in the world, the lust of the flesh, and the lust of the eyes, and the pride of life, is not of the Father, but is of the world. And the world passes away, and the lust thereof: but he that does the will of God abides forever."*

How do you feel? (Answer the following questions):

> Growing up did our parents help you when you were struggling emotionally? How would they respond? (For instance, they were uncomfortable with our feelings so they would quickly tell me what to do.)

_____

_____

> Were you able to share our feelings with our brother or sister? Or did you have to talk to friends about our feelings. (for instance, our friends cared more about how you felt than our siblings).

_____

_____

Balanced Love Dependence

Developing Spiritual Well-Being:

To really examine what it means to have a sense of spiritual our well-being. You must understand that it doesn't come from having knowledge alone, you'll find it only as you appeal through prayer, to God for transformation and requesting for His intervention. The principle within (Job 31:6) suggests this, *"Let me be weighed in an even balance, that God may know my integrity."*

- ✓ First, to find our spiritual well-being you must accept the ugly reality that as humans we are unreliable and prone to make mistakes.

- ✓ Second, acknowledge our own inability to solve all our problems. Meaning that when you attempt to stabilize our emotions through our own efforts, you simply do not have what it takes to find His peace.

- ✓ Third, yield our self-will to the will of God and let our lives be guided by His wisdom.

- ✓ Finally, as you develop spiritual our well-being, you make the choice to allow healthy characteristics to develop.

Step 5. Who's In Control?

Can you summarize our life with a single statement? Everywhere I turn I feel controlled by something I can do absolutely nothing about!" I feel controlled!!!

Questionnaire:

____ When I grew up I was expected to obey the rules with no questions asked.

____ I would like to speak more freely about my personal feelings, but to do so would only lead to arguments or disappointments.

____ When I share my opinion or preference, its often putdown or not accepted.

____ The people I'd like to be most open with are not always available to talk with.

____ I feel as if I live with critics.

____ Peacefulness only happens when I can get away by myself.

____ I often have to choose my words carefully when I'm around certain people.

_____ I've lost some friends because of long periods of time not talking with one another.

_____ I often feel that the things that I do are what people judge me on and is the only thing that matters to them.

_____ I have stressful relationships with friends and family members.

Control is not always bad; structure and organization are needed in our life as indicated within this principle. (1 Peter 2:13-14) *"Submit ourselves to every ordinance of man for the Lord's sake: whether it be to the king, as supreme; Or to governors, as to them that are sent by him for the punishment of evil doers, and for the praise of them that do well."*

How Does Control Occur?

Controlling behavior is shown in a variety of ways. The most obvious ways are bossiness, criticism, stubbornness, dogmatic communication, and chronic rebuttal. But control is an extremely broad trait; it can be shown by unavailability, silence, lack of concern, argumentative, and ultra-sensitivity.

There is one outstanding factor that stands out when people display controlling behaviors that is; when **their threatened by differentness.**

Most controlling people consider themselves open-minded enough to allow others to be different. However, while they give themselves credit for being open-minded, their lives don't reflect this tolerance. Emphases on predictability within relationships and insistence upon the other person to become more like them are typical indicators of a controlling person's inability to accept difference.

The principle within (Psalm 139:14*) "I will praise You: for I am fearfully and wonderfully made: marvelous are Our works: and that my soul knows right well."* God's never intended for everyone and everything to be the same; instead we are to blend our differentness in complementary ways. This is shown in the variety of colors, sights, sounds, animals, plants, feelings, faces and personalities. A lack of differences would create a truly miserable world.

Responses to Being Controlled

<u>Power Struggles</u>: (Negative Response)

People that feel controlled by another person often make attempts to free themselves from the individual through some sort of counter-control method. Example: engaging in power struggles to declare their position of one that is different, uncontrollable or independent.   Most often this approach invites conflict and power playing within the relationship. (Prov. 15:1) *"A soft answer turns away wrath, but a harsh word stirs up anger."* This principle suggests that you do not have to be subject to abusive language or controlling behavior nor do you have to revert to becoming abusive or controlling yourself. Rather, it means you can choose to behave appropriately in the face of another's inappropriateness.

Innate Right to Freedom: (Positive Response)

To break the grip of another person's control and to stop from becoming controlling ourselves, you must acknowledge that each human is given freedom-the presence of choices. Freedom is indigenous to who you are. You don't have to beg for it, nor do you have to prove yourself first. It is simply a part of who you are.

GOD is the ONE who should be in control. People are to resist from the temptation to play God. (James 4:7)

"Submit ourselves therefore to God. Resist the devil, and he will flee from you." When people are controlling, they ignore this most basic principle given at creation, negating another's privilege of freedom and taking the position of God upon themselves.

*Ideally, in freedom you choose to manage our anger by using one of the two healthy choices discussed in the (2nd step), assertiveness or dropping it.

Step 6. Truth or Fiction about Me

(John 16:13) *"Howbeit when he, the spirit of truth, is come, he will guide you into all truth: for he shall not speak of himself; but whatsoever he shall hear, that shall he speak: and will show you things to come."*

Fiction: <u>Because I've been rejected by others for so long, I'm always going to feel emotionally defeated.</u>

Truth: Because anger is so closely related to experiences of rejection, it's common to assume that you are forever jinxed if they have felt rejected several times. ["No one will accept me, so I've got the right to be angry"]. Most of us know that you are not going to be accepted by all people all the time. However, they are not prepared emotionally for the fact that many people may not accept them at all. (2 Corinthians 12:9) *"And He said to me, My grace is sufficient for you: for My strength is made perfect in weakness. Most gladly therefore will I rather glory in my infirmities, that the power of Christ may rest upon me."*

Fiction: A loving God wouldn't have let this happen.

Truth: Anger is usually a by-product of some form of pain. When you attempt to find the root of that pain, God is too often blamed. (1 Corinthians 10:13) *"There has no temptation taken you but such as is common to man: but God is faithful, who will not suffer you to be tempted, above that you are able: but will with the temptation also make a way to escape, that you may be able to bear it."*

Fiction: "Letting it go" is cowardly.

Truth: In (step 2) we discussed ways you can assertively address issues related to worth, needs, and morals. And, if these didn't work, then you still have the choice to drop the anger altogether, opting for forgiveness or acceptance of imperfection. Many angry people find this choice difficult. (Philippians 4:13*) "I can do all things through Christ which strengthens me."*

Fiction: No one understands my problems.

Truth: When have you felt that no one could understand our frustrating circumstances? Most angry people have held on to deep feelings of pain in private, which feeds the myth that no one can understand them. But when they learn to be open about their needs and let others show concern for them, the anger gives way to feelings of relief.

Fiction: <u>I don't deserve to be happy.</u>

Truth: Have you ever asked yourself the question; "How can I feel right about being happy when someone is in so much pain? It's not uncommon to experience emotions like this, however you need not feel obligated to take responsibility for others problems, nor do you have to be sojourners with them in their misery.

The principle within (Prov. 3:13) reinforces the importance for a person to gain understanding and apply the recommended steps to achieve success in managing the emotions attached to anger *"Happy is the man that findeth wisdom, and the man that getteth understanding."*

Fiction: I have nothing to look forward to anymore.

Truth: This same mindset can work against you in anger management. When people have a pattern of problems or issues, it's easy for them to conclude that their future will be no different. Anger can cause people to falsely conclude that trying to correct it or change will be pointless.

To counter this way of thinking, the person must make the decision to renew their way of thinking. The principle within (Ephesians 4:23-24) *"And be renewed I the spirit of our mind; And that you put on the new man, which after God is created in righteousness and true holiness."* Certainly would apply. (To do this, the person must purpose within themselves that they are going to have the kind of mentality that God intended; (Jeremiah 29:11) *"For I know the thoughts that I think toward you, says the Lord, thoughts of peace, and not of evil, to give you an expected end."*

Part Three:
How Other Emotions Create Anger

Step 7. Self-Created Anger

When most people try to determine the reasons for their anger, they point to <u>external</u> pressure; my parents neglected my basic needs, my job is stressful, my friends don't know how to relate to me etc. These types of external circumstances can have an effect on how you think of yourself. The Apostle Paul also writes (Romans 8:1) *"There is therefore now no condemnation to them which are in Christ Jesus who walk not after the flesh, but after the Spirit."* Self-Created Anger can best be describe within the following six descriptions.

<u>Are You Setting Yourself up for failure?</u>

1). <u>Pushing aside your Morals:</u> Remember that anger is connected to the protection of our personal worth, needs, and morals. And when a person is not affirmed by others they compromise their morals to gain acceptance. (Questionnaire)

Check the following statements that apply to you to help decide if morality problems play a role in our anger.

____ I hold onto lustful thoughts and fantasies more often than I should.

____ When I'm with my friends, I become easily tempted to participate in activities I should probably avoid.

____ I find myself questioning the way that I was raised, in my family.

____ There are times when I feel like two different people, a public good person and a private devious, conniving, hate filled person.

____ Going to my place of worship is more of a ritual than a truly purposeful experience.

____ I enjoy obscene, offensive dirty jokes or stories.

____ I have to struggle to maintain purity in my sexual habits.

____ I don't see anything thing wrong with cheating, if it gets me what I want.

____ I would rather go party at a nightclub all night than spend a quiet evening at home.

____ I had several social relationships that began with excitement but ended in frustration.

Ultimately, morality is a reflection of our respect for yourself and others. It illustrates belief in the dignity of other human beings including you. Immorality gives people a sense of meaninglessness, and blame.

2). <u>Consumed by work</u>: When people become consumed by work and busyness they typically describe themselves as stressed. **Stress** has been used as a term that deflects us from recognizing the anger that is a part of it. Overworked, stressful people are more likely to become angry. **Spiritual Balance** is the remedy for stress. The principles referred to in the book of (Matthew 6:24-34) speaks to the reader about the dangers of living our life without spiritual balance and relying on God rather than self when it comes to control things in our life.

"No man can serve two masters: for either he will hate the one, and love the other; or else he will hold to the one, and despise the other. Ye cannot serve God and mammon.

Therefore I say unto you, Take no thought for our life, what ye shall eat, or what ye shall drink; nor yet for our body, what ye shall put on. Is not the life more than meat, and the body than raiment?

Behold the fowls of the air: for they sow not, neither do they reap, nor gather into barns; yet our heavenly Father feedeth them. Are ye not much better than they?

Which of you by taking thought can add one cubit unto his stature?

And why take ye thought for raiment? Consider the lilies of the field, how they grow; they toil not, neither do they spin:

And yet I say unto you, That even Solomon in all his glory was not arrayed like one of these.

Wherefore, if God so clothe the grass of the field, which to day is, and to morrow is cast into the oven, shall he not much more clothe you, O ye of little faith?

Therefore take no thought, saying, What shall we eat? or, What shall we drink? or, Wherewithal shall we be clothed?

(For after all these things do the Gentiles seek:) for our heavenly Father knoweth that ye have need of all these things.

But seek ye first the kingdom of God, and his righteousness; and all these things shall be added unto you.

Take therefore no thought for the morrow: for the morrow shall take thought for the things of itself. Sufficient unto the day is the evil thereof."

3). <u>Physical & Emotional Health</u>:

Excessive drinking, lack of exercise, eating fatty foods, repeated dieting, smoking and lack of proper rest can play a role in self-created anger. Each of these habits contributes to irritability or low self-esteem and reduces our quality of life.

Our emotional & physical healthiness strongly affects our feelings. People seeking to manage anger properly will correctly conclude that physical health is not an isolated factor, but a powerful component of personal stability.

4). <u>Coveting</u>: The most common type of anger associated with material gain is jealousy and envy over

possessions. If you covet or are obsessed with obtaining all of the materialistic items you seek, you are in danger of developing a false superiority. And if you are not able to obtain the material that you seek you become open to discouragement.

How do you feel? (Check below):

____ I have a great desire to appear successful.

____ I often put on false front, hoping to create a good impression.

____ I sometimes indulge fantasies of what it might be like "at the top."

____ If I achieve something or buy something new I want people to notice.

____ I keep score of my own gains in comparison to the gains of friends and family.

____ I feel frustrated because I haven't received the same lucky breaks as someone else.

____ I spend too much money on things such as clothes or cars to the extent that I put myself in dept.

Envious people are extremely competitive, and often look down or condemn others. If another person has more, he or she is the target of criticism about the way they became successful. If a person has less, the envious person has a sense of satisfaction at that person's expense.

5). <u>Abusing Substances</u>: Substance abuse is usually easy to explain by citing peer pressure, wanting to feel valued by their peers, and crossing the line of good moral judgment.

But more is involved in substance abuse than just peer pressure or habit or pleasure. Although substance abuse allows you to escape our problems temporarily, it usually increases ill will in our closest relationships. The alternative to substance abuse is open, constructive communication about personal needs. The principle in (Galatians 6:2) *"Bear one another's burdens, and so fulfill the law of Christ."* Rather than hiding from the hard work of exploring emotions, committing yourself to long-term problem solving will lead to lifetime of reward.

6). <u>Lack of Spiritual Development</u>: To ignore our spiritual life is to deny or not accept our absolute unique relationship with God (Genesis 1:27) *"God created man in His own image, in the image of God created He him; male and female created He them."* And to other creatures as their divinely appointed stewards (Psalms 8:5-8) *"For You have made him a little lower than the angels, and have crowned him with glory and honor. You made him to have dominion over the works of our hands: You have put all things under his feet: All sheep and oxen, and the beast of the field; the fowl of the air, and the fish of the sea, and whatsoever passes through the paths of the seas."* Spiritual stability helps you to maintain a relationship with God, our problems becomes less overwhelming, and a sense of worth in God becomes established. Being at peace with God empowers you to confidently combat worldly imperfections.

Developing our spiritual life involves more than attending place of worship regularly. It starts with recognition that relying on God our meaning in life is both essential and desirable. It then follows that you will seek God's will by exploration and committing our lifestyle to His direction. Finally, associate yourself with like-minded people giving and receiving strength in Godly relationships.

Step 8. The Power of Pride

What is Pride?

Pride is the emotion of self-preoccupation that controls our attitudes, which results in, you becoming insensitive and callous towards others, neglecting their personal worth, morals and essential needs. An example of this type of pride was displayed through the King Nebuchadnezzar in (Daniel 5:20) "But when his heart was lifted up, and his mind hardened in pride, he was deposed from his kingly throne, and they took his glory from him:"

Pride is more than just arrogance or conceit, its virtually any unhealthy, nonproductive emotion or behavior that's very influential in our anger.

How do you feel? (Check below):

____ I tend to speculate why people are not as considerate as I think they should be.

____ When someone is insensitive I let it bother me more than it really should.

____ Impatience or edginess overcomes me when people act incompetently.

____ Sometimes I fantasize what life would be like if I could have ideal circumstances.

____ My mood depends on how others show me respect.

____ I get angry when no one understands my point of view.

____ I am known for having a strong personality.

____ When I witness something good in another person's life, my initial reaction is to wish for the same thing in my life.

____ In social circles, I feel the need to keep a clean reputation, so I cover my issues by masking them with a smile.

____ I'd rather keep my personal life to myself.

The Influence of Pride

It is important to understand the influence pride can have on personality and how it's linked to our inborn sinful nature and transmitted to those around us. This nature accompanies all inappropriate forms of anger: you shout or ridicule or criticize or withdraw in abusive silence and wonder, why can't people be what I say they should be?

Accepting that pride is a part of our inborn sinful nature, you accept the fact that you can prevent the transmission and how it affects others. Also, not blaming anyone else for its presence in our life, taking full responsible for it. Remember, our effort will be lifelong, just when you think you have mastered pride it will reappear. Our commitment to humility needs to be repeated daily.

Purpose of Humility

Because pride is so closely linked to our sinful spiritual condition, the only way to manage it spiritual is by choosing Humility. This is the trait that keeps us in submission to God and is the complete opposite of self-preoccupation and a willingness to acknowledge our personal limits.

Pride, as the emotion of self-preoccupation, can become the all-consuming drive that a person becomes obsessed about how others can and should respond to them. When you worry too much about the effect of another person's behavior on our life you respond too sensitively when a need is ignored. (Matthew 6:44-47) *"But I say to you, Love our enemies, bless them that curse you, do good to them that hate you, and pray for them which spitefully use you, and persecute you; That you may be the children of our Father which is in heaven: for He makes His sun to rise on the evil and on the good, and sends rain on the just and the unjust. For if you love them which love you, what reward have you? Do not even the publicans the same? And if you salute our brethren only, what do you more than others? Do not even the publicans so?"*

Selfishness can become so natural, you must consciously tune in to others. This requires you to be sensitive to others feeling and to recognize that their differing perceptions can have full validity.

Acknowledging Self - limits

No matter how brilliant we think we are, we do have limits. By continuing to try to push or force our preferences and ideas on to others you create trouble, **attempting to play the "God role" in someone life is not only dangerous but it oversteps the boundaries that God established between Him and us as humans**. Anger management requires you to *willingly* recognize our own personal limits and accept pain and imperfection within others.

How do you feel? (Check below):
___ I can handle and respect the fact that many people will have a different opinion from me.

____ When someone makes a mistake, it is not my position to criticize or judge.

____ I stop myself from giving advice or suggestions when I know they won't be appreciated anyway.

____ I am aware that no one needs to take my advice or suggestions

____ I accept the fact that pain will exist in my life

Does being humble mean that I can't say what's on my mind?

The answer is No. Recall in (step 2), positively and assertively expressing our anger emotion is a healthy choice. (Col. 4:6) *"Let our speech be always with grace, as though seasoned with salt so that you may know how to answer each person."* In turn, this principle suggests you realize that the choice of humility indicates that you've accepted our own limits and have decided to set aside self-preoccupations.

Step 9. The Consequences of Fear

Fear implies a condition marked by feelings of doubt, worry and uncertainty. It's an emotion that stops us from living with complete confidence. To the opposite of this point, Paul explained, (Romans 8:15) *"For ye have not received the spirit of bondage again to fear; but ye have received the Spirit of adoption, whereby you cry, Abba, Father."* (adoption means the inherent right, and Abba is Aramaic for "Father").

To be able to set fears aside, it's good to understand what creates them and why you struggle with it. Here are three possibilities to discuss:

1. Personalizing Rejection:

When you over personalize rejections, or apply false statements to our self-esteem, you are not only guilty of letting others have too much power, you also are communicating "I can't trust myself." This lack of self-trust, when noticed by others, gives them idea or assume "permission" to take advantage.

The way to combat this is to hold firmly to our inner morals rather than giving into someone else's agenda. Being assertive, being anchored in the confidence that you are a legitimate person with legitimate needs. You don't have to let another's rejection be the final word.

2. Being Uncertain of Other's Motives:

Fear exists because of the unknowns in other persons' personalities. Can you really trust this person? When they say they love you, can you be sure? When you look at others suspiciously you maintain an edge of selfishness. Our self-preservation mode kicks in and you interpret others motives with cynicism.

To combat this, letting go of our shock associated with fear you will be guided by objectivity. This will allow you to respond without preexisting assumptions about the treatment you should receive.

3. You Forget God Is In Charge:

When our emotions depend on the opinions of others, you are fearful because you can never be sure when you might be rejected or criticized or ignored. As humans, our self-image is only as secure as the humans you entrust with our emotions. But God-based self-image is different. Because God accepts you, weakness and all, you can live with confidence knowing that He can guide you through all relational or circumstantial pitfalls.

Drawing upon Spiritual Strength requires a Spiritual-focus rather than a human focus. You can choose to let our emotions be dictated by humans' opinions or God's opinion. Which will you choose?

Defensiveness Caused by Fear

The emotion of fear is aroused in you through anticipation of pain, anxiety and dread. It keeps you from being fully honest about who you causes you to continue the need to present an image that you feel is more socially acceptable by pretending.

Types of Defenses:

1. **Denial:** This is the refusal to acknowledge personal problems. In most cases denial is subconscious; avoiding issues is so important to the person's character it occurs without thinking.

2. **Evasiveness:** Is different from denial in that evasiveness is driven by a conscious element of fear, while denial involves subconscious self-deception. Evasiveness is a deliberate deception of others. When you act evasively you are specifically choosing to avoid the responsibility of meeting problems head on.

3. **Reversal:** The third general style of defensiveness is more openly combative. The person thinks that the best way to protect themselves is to keep others on the defensive. The reversal technique makes you assume that others are out to get you, so you become offensive whenever self-worth is challenged.

Step 10. Anger as a Result of Loneliness

From the beginning of time God intended for you to maintain close ties with family and friends. This is declared (Gen. 2:18) *"And the Lord God said, it is not good that the man should be alone; I will make him a help meet for him."* Gods' original intent holds true today. You are not created to be alone.

Feeling connected with others is important and without this feeling, loneliness would make you feel vulnerable, defenseless, at risk, or exposed.

Loneliness is the emotion of isolation. It is the empty feeling that comes when you sense a companion is having difficulty relating to our feelings. It makes you aware that gaps exist in our relationships." To be lonely, you don't have to sit in a dark room staring into space.

How do you feel? (Check below):

___ At times I feel I don't really fit in.

___ I sometimes complain that the people in my life don't really understand me.

___ I find myself wanting to be with someone other than the person I am with.

___ Acceptance from others does not come very often.

___ Something seems to be missing in my relationships.

___ In conversations with my friends, I'm unable to discuss my emotions.

___ I become frustrated because I seem to work harder at keeping relationships going than my friends or relatives do.

___ People who know me in public don't really see how I struggle within myself with painful wounds or hurts.

___ The people I want to be closest to do not share the same goals and dreams as I do.

The Causes of Feeling Lonely

Sin Separates

The principle within (James 4:17) defines the term "sin", I think in its simplest form *"Therefore to him that knoweth to good, and doeth it not, to him it is sin."* Ultimately, loneliness is the emotion of feeling estranged from God and therefore prevents you from fully knowing and experiencing contentment. Evidence of one of the first emotional consequences of sin was loneliness. In fear, (Genesis 3:7-10) Adam hid from God. He was ashamed to reveal himself fully. Looking for ways to cover up his vulnerabilities, he became evasive and attempted to isolate himself from the presence of God.

But it must be understood that this was never Gods intent, He instilled love, joy, peace and patience in both Adam and Eve which gave them the feeling of connection with God. This is reinforced the importance (Romans 8:39) *"Nor height, nor depth, nor any other creature, shall be able to separate us from the love of God, which is in Christ Jesus our Lord."*

There will be times when you feel isolated from others. If you choose to accept our circumstances, anger will follow and our emotional pain will increase. Or you can choose to accept the unfortunate imperfection while also resolving to maintain contact with others as best you can. By realizing or accepting the reality of loneliness and that this emotion is an inborn part of us, you will be able to cope and manage the anger that's associated with it much better.

Neglecting Relationships

While loneliness can partially be explained by our sinful nature, loneliness can also be partially blamed on neglected relationships. You can be so busy with work and activities that you put too little attention to more important things, such as empathy or authenticity or bearing burdens.

Being too busy is not the only way to neglect relational growth. You can also be lazy about putting the energy necessary to maintaining a satisfactory relationship with others.

Step 11. The Inferiority Condition

The awareness that you do not measure up to Gods standards causes the tendency to feel inferior, at times. Choosing to participate in a sinful act could lead towards a condition of not being able to meet those standards. (James 4:17) states *"Therefore to him that knoweth to do good, and doeth it not, to him it is sin."* Not all of us are spiritually minded enough to connect feelings of inferiority to our position with God, but each person has wondered at some time, as pointed out in the principle (Job 13:2) *"What you know, the same do I know also. I am not inferior to you."* This was the response Job gave to his friends who were attempting to give him advice and Job reinforced to them, his personal relationship with God and told them that he would speak with the Almighty and reason with God himself.

Despite others good intensions, there will be a time for you to establish a personal spiritual relationship with God and reassure others that our totally and completely dependent upon Him.

- Two traps that should be avoided when dealing with the inferiority condition and attempting to be more superior to others.

(1). Believing that you are Inferior because of personal inadequacies:

Based upon the condition of our mindset, you begin to entertain thoughts of being inferior. Believing that our inadequacies makes you inferior to others. God created men and women equal to one another. We can only be inferior to Him because, of course, He's God!

(2). Seeking False Superiority:

This too is a common trap when seeking an edge or upper hand into not feeling inferior. In attempting to establish superiority, you may obtain a temporary sense of relief but never succeed in totally eliminating the feelings of inferiority.

Treating Others Equally

To avoid the inferior – superior trap, you must admit that you are all equal in human value. As simple as this may seem, it's hard to understand because you resist being grouped under a label perceived as "ordinary."

Ending Judgments

To be obsessed with judging others, you feel compelled to judge the performance of other people. Our appetite towards judging is so great we don't allow ourselves to be who you are.

The attempt to judge or compare one another is a waste of energy. When you apply descriptive thinking you remember that you do not have God-like abilities to properly judge. The writer in (James 4:12) makes this point clear to those that thought that they had the right to judge others *"There is one lawgiver, who is able to save and to destroy: who are you to judge another."*

Part Four:
Applying New Insights

Step 12. New Person

Applying New Our Insights

At this time, you have come full circle in our efforts to managing our anger. Our mind should be awakened and conditioned for a changed pattern of living. (Romans 12:2) suggest this, "And be not conformed to this world: but be you transformed by the renewing of our mind, that you prove what is that good, and acceptable, and perfect, will of God."

Open ourselves up to others

Increased friendship and harmony are possible once make the decision to be willing to open yourself up to others with a new attitude towards how you feel and manage our anger. (Matthew 5:9) "Blessed are the peacemakers: for they shall be called the children of God." This principle lets you know that it's okay to become a new person and for you to reject our former anger emotions that lead to toxic emotional atmospheres of rejection, and self-centeredness that left everyone feeling dissatisfied.

How do you feel? (Check below):

___ I want to be known as someone who finds good in others.

___Doing good has become feels more satisfying.

___I won't become worried when my day becomes hectic; life's too short to remain chronically anxious.

___I can be patient because I am at peace with myself.

___It's only fair that I accept other's imperfections, just as I want them to accept mine.

___I find peace in the small things, such as playing with my kids at the playground, quiet dinner with family members or spending a day with friends.

Damage Control

Unfortunately, the by-product of our former misguided anger damaged relationships, families, Business partnerships, friendships and even within our place of worship fellowships have suffered and the fear of rejected might have made it too difficult to make apologize. While there are no guarantees, you can proceed with a clean future when you are willing to take the lead in our commitments to emotional healthiness.

To truly find balance you must be willing to apologize to those who have been hurt by our past behavior and attitudes. You have to become the person willing to bear no grudges, and be honest about the hurt and pain you have felt. (Matt.6:14, 15) encourages us to forgive others as God has forgiven you. "For if you forgive men of his trespasses, our heavenly Father will also forgive our trespasses. But if you forgive not men their trespasses, neither will our Father forgive our trespasses."

Create a list of people that you think our anger has caused pain and ask for their forgiveness:

_____

_____

_____.

Choose to Be Positive in Our Communication

Once you've understood the meaning and underlying causes of our anger, you can develop goals that will reflect changes of our heart. You can reestablish a reputation as someone who is caring rather than someone that holds on to anger.

Check the following sentences that express our desires for a changed life.

____ I'd like to develop a greater reputation as an encouraging, supportive person.

____ I know I need to be less critical and friendlier with family and friends.

____ Having an open minded approach toward others lifestyle interests.

____ Focusing on what is right and good will take priority over harping on what is wrong.

____ When I'm with others I want to set an upbeat tone or initiate friendly exchange.

____ I want to be more truthful and realistic about myself, with no more games of phoniness or covering up.

____ Rather than getting upset about small things, I intend to give them less attention.

____ True joy with laughter and fellowship with friends and family is what I want.

____ I intend to be less demanding and more flexible as I learn to accept others for who they are.

____ I'll be a better listener and won't be consumed with myself

Ephesians 4:31 tells us *"put away all bitterness, wrath, anger, clamor, and evil speaking, along with all malice." This principle also instructs us to be kind, tenderhearted, and forgiving towards others.*

Conclusion

It's important to remind yourself to embrace the realism of anger within our life and that taking personal ownership is the beginning of improved quality of life. Through the application of these biblical principles, you will begin to notice improved balance of our emotional and spiritual well-being.

The final principle to share as you've completed the 12th step of our journey is (Galatians 6:1-2), which encourages you to help others after you have gained the ability to manage the anger in our life, through witnessing to them how you've become not just a hearer but a doer as well. *"Brethren, if any man be overtaken in a fault, you which are spiritual, restore such a one in the spirit of meekness; considering thyself, lest you also be tempted."*

<u>References</u>

Anger Research Consortium; American Psychological Association

Second College Edition, The American Heritage Dictionary.

Strong, James. *Strong's Exhaustive Concordance of the Bible.* King James 2007

Authorized King James Version. *The Holy Bible...* 2001

<u>Contact Information</u>

www.marvinpricejr.com

Marvin.price61@gmail.com

Journey12step@gmail.com